IMAGES
of America

WESTFIELD

IN THE GOLDEN AGE OF
POSTCARDS

The Plaza and E. Broad Street, *c.* 1923. With the construction of the World War I memorial, Westfield began to look very much as it appears today. (Photograph by Theodore Hintz)

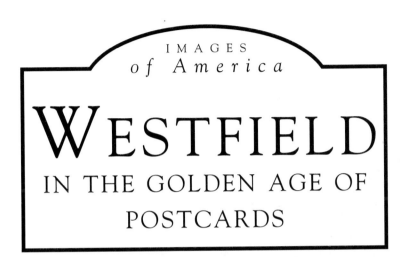

IMAGES
of America

WESTFIELD

IN THE GOLDEN AGE OF
POSTCARDS

Stanley H. Lipson

ARCADIA

First published 1996
Copyright © Stanley H. Lipson, 1996

ISBN 0-7524-0406-7

Published by Arcadia Publishing,
an imprint of the Chalford Publishing Corporation
One Washington Center, Dover, New Hampshire 03820
Printed in Great Britain

To Jody:
Together we have nurtured children,
planted trees, and written a book,
all in Westfield.

Broad Street, c. 1906. The hitching posts have long since disappeared, and the dirt road has been paved, but looking east from the street in front of the Presbyterian church there is a familiar dip in the road near the outlet of the pond.

Contents

The Glens, *c*. 1907.

Introduction

In 1890 the township of Westfield had a population of 2,739. The town of Westfield was incorporated in 1903 and by 1915 had a population of 8,147, concentrated in a fraction of the former area. The intervening years saw the foundation of the town's infrastructure. That period brought a new firehouse, a municipal water system, fire hydrants, a sewer system, parks, and road improvements. Electricity came to Westfield, and with it telephones and trolleys. The town added new schools, a library, and a town hall. The railroad built new train stations. People built homes and churches and recreational facilities. Business flourished. The changed form of government was both a cause and an effect of this development. The increase in taxes caused those living in the outlying districts of the township to complain about the taxes they were paying for services that would not extend out to them. The borough of Mountainside was among the last to split from Westfield. As the town decreased in size and grew in population, the concentration of available funds increased and the first quarter of the twentieth century witnessed unprecedented growth.

This period of time coincided with the "golden age" of postcards. Everything new was proudly documented—rarely were hundred-year-old homes shown. A young Westfield photographer by the name of Karl Baumann received a view camera from relatives in Germany who were in the printing business. They suggested that there was good profit to be made in publishing postcards. Negatives of photographs taken in the United States were sent to Germany where the most modern printing technology in the world produced the cards that were shipped back to this country. Baumann is responsible for a very large number of early images of Westfield and is the primary reason that the number of postcards of the town was disproportionate to its size. Thanks to Baumann and other photographers, the growth and development of the town during its formative years was uniquely captured in the souvenirs sent by residents and visitors to their friends and relatives in all parts of the country. Over the years, postcard collectors searching antique stores, flea markets, and estate sales have managed to locate, identify, and return many of these images to Westfield. Of course, not every facet of town life was recorded on postcards, and undoubtedly there are many cards that have not yet been found. Nevertheless, on the pages that follow will be found a remarkable collection of images that give a fascinating glimpse of an era gone by.

Acknowledgments

Many people have helped bring this book to fruition. Even before there was the idea of a book there was a postcard collection. Phyllis Van Hecke and her late husband George, good friends who delighted in the history of Westfield, made collecting a pleasure and encouraged the documentation of the postcards. Phyllis has loaned the gems of her collection to be shared with the readers of this book. They are marked PVH. The late Kurt Bauer, publisher of the *Westfield Leader*, devoted a portion of his resources and his newspaper to Westfield's history. From time to time he published postcard images, and it was his specific suggestion that led to this book. Cards borrowed from the Westfield Memorial Library are marked WML. Members of the board of the Westfield Historical Society have been especially supportive in encouraging this project. They have been most generous in sharing their incomparable collection, and their cards are marked WHS.

Every effort has been made to give accurate descriptions of the images. In that effort the entire reference staff of the library has been extremely helpful, not to mention patient and understanding. Special thanks must be given to Ralph Jones of the Westfield Historical Society, who generously shared his knowledge of Westfield with the author, as he does with the entire town. His support has been particularly gratifying.

One
Transportation

A Country Road, c. 1907. Wagons and carriages were the most common method of traveling between town and this house, which is still visible on Lamberts Mill Road and Kirkview Circle. One of the few pre-Revolutionary homes shown on a postcard, it was probably built by John Acken, whose son William sold it to John Radley in 1815.

Frank Faulkner, c. 1908. Faulkner Drive is named for Frank, who owned a dairy farm toward the end of Rahway Avenue. He is shown here with his wagon and team. (PVH)

Dudley Avenue, c. 1906. It was not just the farms that depended on horse power. Deliveries throughout the town were made by wagon. All of the larger homes in town had carriage houses, many of which still exist today. In the snows of winter people merely switched to a sleigh.

The Carriage Factory, c. 1906. Hiram L. Fink and his workers built and repaired "fine carriages, business wagons, and sleighs" in his Elm Street shop. As automobiles became popular, the business became the Westfield Garage, now a municipal parking lot across the street from the Texaco gas station. Fink's telephone number was 2-F. (PVH)

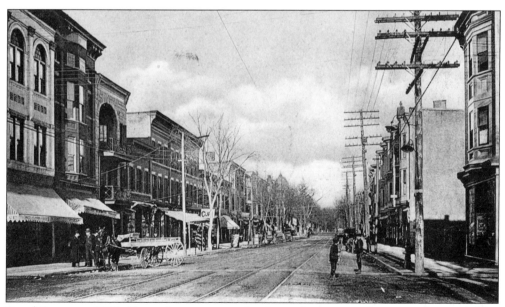

Broad Street, c. 1905. Horse-drawn wagons dominate the business district in this view from Prospect Street to Elm Street. The photographer erased the overhead wires from the trolley but left the telephone poles. The first telephone exchange was in the rear of William Trenchard's Westfield Pharmacy, the first building on the left.

Railroad Station, c. 1907. Commuters returning on the evening train found carriages waiting to take them home. The railroad had come to Westfield as early as 1838, but it was not until the 1870s that the Central Railroad of New Jersey began providing direct service to Jersey City with a connecting ferry to New York. (Baumann)

Railroad Station, c. 1908. The Central built the current northside station in 1892. In order to increase business the railroad actively promoted home ownership in Westfield and the convenient train ride to New York. By 1900 approximately one of every eight residents commuted daily.

Railroad Station, c. 1906. One of the factors contributing to the great variety of Westfield's postcards was their use by the railroad in promoting the town. The Central used the American News Company's kiosks and newsstands at its stations to market the cards.

The East Bound Station, c. 1909. The southside station was added after the turn of the century. Prior to that, riders had to purchase their tickets and dash across the tracks to catch the train.

Broad Street from Methodist Church,
Westfield, N. J.

Broad Street Traffic, c. 1907. Almost all of the buildings in this photograph are still here, but trucks today don't have to share the road with horse-drawn wagons or the Main Line trolley. On the near corner, the awning over James Casey's store proclaims "Segars," while the sign below his window advertises Fritz's Ice Cream. Across the street Louis Dughi's store has signs for Moxie, 5¢ Owl Cigars, Coke Cola, Ice Cream, and Soda Water. Just in front of the trolley car is the awning of Woodruff's Market. A "Stop" sign hangs from the trolley wires at the corner of Prospect Street. The trolley tracks entered Westfield from Scotch Plains along Brightwood Avenue and, turning at Prospect, crossed over Newton Place to Elm Street. They turned again at Broad Street to about the point from which this picture was taken and crossed under the railroad tracks to South Avenue. From there they turned and followed Summit Avenue to Grove, turning one final time on their way to Garwood. Car barns were located at the intersection of Grove and Boynton Avenue, and at that point a branch line headed off to Rahway. Understandably, a significant proportion of the town's growth took place within walking distance of the trolley tracks, and most of the shops, schools, and recreational facilities were accessible by trolley.

An Electric Truck, c. 1910. Before gasoline became the dominant fuel of the twentieth century, Eldamora Lawrence posed with one of the first electric trucks in front of his grocery market at 140 Broad Street.

Broad Street, c. 1908. To the right is the awning of Scheuer & Sons, groceries. Just beyond is a sign for a public telephone, and the sign at the curb by the cyclist says "New York Candy Kitchen—Ice Cream and Soda Water." Many of the buildings in this view looking from Elm Street toward Prospect Street are still standing.

The Horse-Drawn Empire Engine, c. 1907. Engine Company #1, a unit of the town's fire department, pose in front of the original wooden firehouse that stood by the train station on the same site as the current building. (PVH)

The Webb Pumper. In 1911 Westfield became the first town in Union County to obtain a motor-driven fire truck. The fire department continued to use horses to pull its equipment until 1922, when the last horse-drawn ladder truck was replaced and the last horse was retired. (WHS)

The Westfield Dairy, c. 1908. John Dickson's dairy was on E. Broad Street opposite what is now the parking lot at the corner of Mountain Avenue. The dairy was between the old library to the left and the site where the Rialto Theater would eventually be built. Horse-drawn wagons delivered the milk, which was cooled by ice cut from the pond. (WHS)

Viswat's Dairy, c. 1943. Thirty-five years later, Viswat's Dairy had its own gas pump to supply its modern dairy truck. The building, located at 1010 South Avenue, has been extensively renovated, and the front has been modified to accommodate several retail establishments.

Elm and Broad Streets, c. 1912. For many years the horse and the gasoline engine coexisted peaceably. There seems to have been an abundance of parking spaces as well. (Baumann)

The Underpass at the Plaza, c. 1923. As traffic increased, it became apparent that the level grade crossing at Broad Street was becoming more and more hazardous. In 1919 the trolley tunnel was relocated to the west and widened to create the underpass and the plaza. (PVH)

Public Library, Westfield   N. J.

The Library, *c*. 1928. By the late 1920s the automobile had become not merely a novelty, but an important means of transporting people from one part of town to another.

East Broad from Elm, *c*. 1928. By the time this photograph was taken, cars totally dominated Broad Street. Nevertheless, the trolley would remain important for a few more years.

Elm Street, *c*. 1912. This is the intersection at Walnut Avenue. Several years later the portion to the left was renamed for Harold Cowperthwaite, who was killed in World War I. The building to the right with the distinctive roof is easily recognizable today. (PVH)

Elm Street from Dudley, *c*. 1914. Rubber-tired trolleys replaced the tracked vehicles in 1935, and they were replaced by buses in 1947. The tracks along Elm Street were removed and used for scrap. When the street was resurfaced in recent years, residents were surprised to learn that the ties had been left in place and merely paved over.

Two

Schools

Washington School Festivities. Onlookers watch as teachers direct children dressed for a pageant. (WHS)

A Souvenir of Westfield, *c.* 1905. Before late 1907 it was not legal to write anything but an address on the back of a postcard. By using vignettes of the Washington and Lincoln Schools, the publisher left space on the front for the sender to place a brief message.

A Group of Schools, *c.* 1909. This card was produced shortly after McKinley School was opened in 1908. It also shows the Prospect and Lincoln Schools. (PVH)

Prospect School, *c.* 1908. This school was built in 1869 where the municipal parking lot is currently located on Prospect Street. It was used as an elementary school until 1916 and as a high school for three years after that. (Schaefer & Frutchey)

3888   Washington School.   Westfield N. J.

Washington School, *c.* 1910. The original Washington School was built in 1900 facing Elm Street between Orchard Street and Walnut Street. The park in front of it, now the Elm Street playground, was often the scene of concerts, assemblies, and pageants. The house to the left of the school can be seen today across the street from the tennis court parking lot.

WASHINGTON SCHOOL. WESTFIELD, N. J.

Washington School, *c.* 1906. Children at recess play a circle game in the playground at Washington School.

24

Lincoln School, *c.* 1906. The first Lincoln School was built in 1890 on Academy (now Temple) Place. The houses to the left of the school can be seen today on the 500 block of Boulevard. Both Washington and Lincoln were located on the trolley line. The school on Prospect was a block from the tracks.

Grant School. Shown here shortly after it opened, Grant School was completed in time for the beginning of classes in September 1912. The school was situated on Stanley Avenue, where the municipal library is currently located.

McKinley School, c. 1908. Westfield's phenomenal population growth required the steady addition of new schools. The quality of the schools helped attract additional residents. This upward spiral continued for the next sixty years.

Westfield's new school built in 1908, costing $40,000 is shown on this card. **It is located on our property, WESTFIELD HIGHLANDS.** We have fine building plots for sale, located on a hill with beautiful views, which we sell at very low prices and on the easiest of monthly payments.

Full but moderate restrictions. Many residents of Westfield have purchased. An early selection will be to your advantage.

H. C. LOCKWOOD
141 Broadway, N. Y.
or 38 Elm St., Westfield, N. J.

McKinley School, 1908. The front of this card shows an artist's rendition of the school while still under construction. Similar messages from H.C. Lockwood have been found typed on the backs of several postcards showing various churches and the train station.

The High School. Built in 1916, the building on the corner of Elm and Walnut Streets initially housed the high school. It continued in that capacity until the new high school was built on Dorian Road in 1952. Shown here just after it opened, the building currently houses the administrative offices of the board of education.

Roosevelt School, c. 1926. Viewed from this angle, the junior high school looks pretty much the same today as it did when it was built in 1926.

Franklin School, 1930. The last of the schools to be built during the postcard era, Franklin is located on Newton Place.

Lincoln School, c. 1925. The new Lincoln School was erected on Westfield Avenue in 1922, just after the old Lincoln School was abandoned. Today the facility is under lease to the Union County Educational Services Commission.

Three

Churches

Broad and Chestnut Streets. WESTFIELD, N. J. Under these trees the first Methodist meeting was held in Westfield, 1849.

Stable

"The Farm"

BAUMANN PHOTO.

Broad and Chestnut Streets, c. 1912. A pre-Revolutionary structure, the Henry Baker House was the scene of a skirmish between the local militia and the British. It was owned by C.A. Leveridge when the Methodists met there in 1849 to organize their church. In recent years the owner demolished it to develop Bradson Court. The former stable is now a home on Saunders Avenue. (Baumann)

A Souvenir of Westfield, *c.* 1905. This early double view shows the Methodist and Congregational churches.

A Group of Churches, *c.* 1909. In addition to transportation and excellent schools, one of the factors contributing to the town's growth has been its graceful churches, ministering to a wide variety of beliefs. This card shows the early Congregational, Baptist, and Episcopalian churches. (PVH)

The white Church

The White Church. The Presbyterian church is the town's oldest, with roots dating from before the Revolutionary War. The present structure, the congregation's fourth, was built in 1862 and has remained a Westfield landmark through the entire twentieth century.

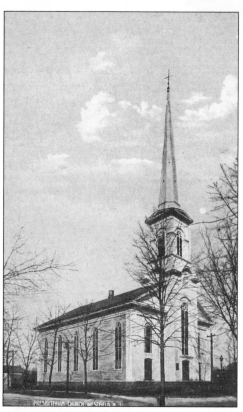

The Presbyterian Church, *c.* 1908. A count of the windows in the building today betrays the fact that a hundred years after it was built, the church was lengthened. It was split just behind the third window, the steeple end was rolled forward, and a new section was inserted. This added two windows and about 30 feet, while preserving the church's original appearance.

The Presbyterian Church and Manse, *c.* 1910. Westminster Hall, dating from 1853, is the oldest building currently on this site. The beautiful Victorian manse, to the right with the wrap-around porches, was built in 1888 and demolished in 1956.

Presbyterian Sunday School, *c.* 1935. Growing with the town, the church erected a new parish house in 1929.

The Willow Grove Chapel, *c.* 1906. Originally located within the boundaries of Westfield, the present building was constructed in 1887 as an adjunct of the Presbyterian church. Today it is known as the Willow Grove Presbyterian Church, located on Raritan Road in Scotch Plains.

The Methodist Episcopal Church, c. 1906. The cornerstone of this church was laid in 1851. In spite of extensive renovation and expansion over the years, the church had difficulty accommodating the needs of the growing town; accordingly, the necessity of building a larger structure was acknowledged and bids were solicited.

The New Projected M. E. Church of Westfield, N. J.

The Projected M.E. Church, c. 1907. How different Westfield would look today if the proposal by architect Charles Granville Jones had been accepted! (Baumann)

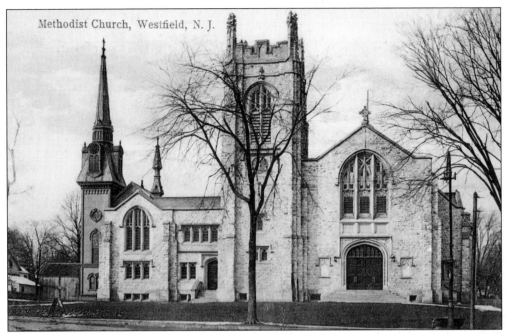

Methodist Churches, 1912. This rare postcard shows the new church just after completion. The old one had been moved back in 1910 so that construction could take place on the same site. (WML)

The Methodist Church, c. 1914. This is an excellent example of Karl Baumann's photographic style. The picture has been taken from a low angle to accentuate the building's proportions, and enough of a tree is shown to suggest a park-like setting. (Baumann)

The Church of Christ, *c*. 1907. The Congregational Church of Christ was organized in 1880 by members of the Presbyterian Church. The original Queen Anne-style house of worship was built on Elmer Street in 1882. As early as 1890 alterations were made to double the seating capacity.

The Congregational Church, *c*. 1906. As with all of the town's institutions, continued growth necessitated continual modification and expansion. Rejecting a 1910 proposal for a stone edifice similar to that which the Methodists were building, they built instead the parish house that is still located on this site. The original church remained in place until the late 1940s.

St. Paul's Church, *c*. 1914. The Episcopal Church, originally known as Grace Church, was organized in 1867. Services were held in several locations before the cornerstone of this building was laid in 1875.

St. Paul's, *c*. 1940s. Looking across the pond toward E. Broad Street, this unusual view shows the church at the corner of St. Paul Street.

The Baptist Church, *c.* 1910. The original Baptist church was on Elm Street on the site of the present church. To the right is the parish house, and beyond that, the top of the Westfield Casino is barely visible. (Baumann)

The Baptist Church, *c.* 1924. The original church was built in 1867 and expanded twenty years later. By 1920 the congregation had outgrown it, and accordingly, the new stone church was built in 1922.

The Holy Trinity R.C. Church, c. 1910. The first Catholic church was built in 1872 on New York Avenue, now Trinity Place. It was a mission church, attended to from Cranford. The appointment of Father Reilly as the first parish priest came in 1903, just as Westfield was becoming a town.

The Roman Catholic Church, c. 1923. Reverend H.J. Watterson came to Westfield in 1913. Under his guidance a parochial school was begun, and, in 1921, ground was broken for a new Holy Trinity Church on Westfield Avenue. Charles A. Philhower, Westfield historian and supervisor of schools, referred to it as a "scholarly example of colonial renaissance architecture."

The Methodist Church. (Photograph by Henry Fullerton)

Four
Entertainment and Recreation

The Excursion, 1903. For many years several of the town's churches sponsored a one-day train trip to Asbury Park. This advertisement for the August 2, 1903 excursion is the earliest known Westfield postcard.

You are invited to visit our Camp. The matron and children will be glad to welcome you at any time

EXECUTIVE COMMITTEE

GEORGE E. WOOLFE
PRESIDENT

LAWRENCE A. CLARK
TREASURER

MRS. GERTRUDE H. DIEHL
MATRON

Camp Woolfe, 1903. Another early card shows the fresh air camp located in the woods near Grove Street and Summit Avenue. Accessible by trolley, it provided outings for "worthy mothers and their sickly children." It was also the site of weekly evangelical services. (PVH)

On the Golf Links, Westfield, N. J.

Did you have a nice time at the Fox Hill Fair? What do you think of our "Golf Links"? This is a portion of Father's "Mae" Real Estate.

On the Golf Links, c. 1908. In 1900 a group of men headed by Edwin R. Perkins of Stoneleigh Park formed the Westfield Golf Club and purchased the Osborn Farm on Old Jerusalem Road. The farm was a few hundred feet over the line into Scotch Plains and was accessible by trolley; it was a 1.5-mile ride from the train station in town.

Golf Club House, Westfield, N. J.

The Clubhouse, c. 1908. The farmhouse was converted to a clubhouse that stands to this day. The course was modified and eventually called "the best nine-hole course in the eastern states." With the addition of courts, tennis became an important activity, and the club became the third in the world to install floodlights for play after dark.

GOLF COURSE
SHADY REST COUNTRY CLUB
WESTFIELD N.J.

The Shady Rest Country Club, c. 1923. With the growth in popularity of 18-hole golf courses, membership declined, and in 1921 the Westfield Club merged with the Cranford Golf Club to form the Echo Lake Country Club. That same year interest in the original property was transferred from the Westfield Golf Club Realty Co. to the Shady Rest Country Club.

The Casino, c. 1908. The Westfield Athletic Club, which had previously met in Gale's Club House, built this facility in 1892. A year later they merged with a local social group to become the Westfield Club. The building was located on Elm Street between the parsonage of the Baptist church and the current entrance to the municipal parking lot. Behind it were the tombstones of the Old Revolutionary Cemetery. In the distance to the right could be seen the rear of the Presbyterian church. For nearly two decades the building served as the center of the town's social and recreational activities. The club disbanded in 1906 and for nearly two years use was limited almost exclusively to individuals who rented the bowling alleys, pool tables, or dance hall. About 1908 the "moving picture craze" swept the town, and, reorganized as the Casino, the building became more popular than ever. Just about every social organization held affairs here. Schools held their closing exercises in the auditorium, which was also the scene of local political conventions. The building was totally destroyed by a spectacular fire in 1911 (see p. 71).

Moving
Pictures

Bowling
Alleys

Pool Tables
Billiards

Tennis
Courts

Westfield's
Leading
Place
of
Amusement

WESTFIELD CASINO

The Casino, 1908. The newly reorganized Casino used this postcard to advertise the availability of its facilities.

The Clubhouse, c. 1906. The tennis courts at the Westfield Club supplemented those at the Westfield Golf Club on Jerusalem Road. The destruction of the Casino and the difficulties the Westfield Golf Club had in providing for both golf and tennis encouraged the formation of the Westfield Tennis Club in 1915.

A Scene from *Officer 666*, 1913. Less than a month after the Casino burned, Walter W. Mooney purchased the property on Elm Street where Gale's Club House had stood to construct an "all fireproof" theater. Opening in January 1913, it had a full-size stage and a seating capacity of about eight hundred. (PVH)

Officer 666. Officer 666 played in Chicago and New York before coming to town for one day on March 29, 1913. (PVH)

POST CARD

SCENE FROM

COHAN & HARRIS'

MELODRAMATIC
FARCE

OFFICER 666

By
AUGUSTIN McHUGH

For Address Only

THE PLAYHOUSE
WESTFIELD
Sat., March 29
Mat. and Night

Postcard Backs, 1913. The fare at the Playhouse was varied. Five days earlier Tyrone Power had appeared in *Julius Caesar* "with a cast of sixty." That was followed by two evenings of The Great Houdon "mystifying audiences in A Night With the Spirits." (PVH)

The Westfield Theater. Directly across the street, Arthur S. Flagg built the Westfield Theater, which opened in 1912. This easily recognizable building was intended primarily to be a movie theater and lecture hall. The assembly hall upstairs was the scene of such events as the Firemen's Ball of 1913.

The Masonic Temple, *c.* 1929. Westfield's Masonic lodge, Atlas #125, had several homes over the years, including the Prospect Street school, Arcanum Hall, and the bank building diagonally opposite. In 1929 they built this rare example of Egyptian Revival architecture on Temple Place. After a fire, it was razed in the 1970s and replaced with housing.

The YMCA, *c.* 1933. Before the turn of the century the YMCA was located in the old Gale Club House on Elm Street. It was reorganized in 1923, and a building campaign was started in 1927. That resulted in the construction two years later of the structure on Ferris Place and Clark Street that, although greatly expanded, still retains its original character.

Five

Trees and Parks

"The Big Oak," Mountain Avenue, *c*. 1910. This tree is mentioned as one of the boundary markers on the old deeds of the Miller-Cory property. It has been removed in recent years, and the board sidewalks have long since been replaced, but the distinctive houses can still be seen where Mountain intersects Dudley Avenue and Raymond Street.

Clark's Pond, *c.* 1907. This postcard is one of two that, when joined, give a panoramic view of what was known as Clark's Pond. The Presbyterian church is in the background.

The Lake, *c.* 1910. Long before the first park, Westfielders valued the town's trees and open spaces. At some times of the year, however, mosquitoes—as well as odors from the old tannery and Peckham's dump near the Mountain Avenue entrance—made the area quite unappealing.

Clark's Pond, c. 1907. Although a separate postcard, this scene is a continuation of the one on the facing page. The town acquired the pond and the surrounding property in 1907 and spent another eight years debating what to do with it.

The Pond, c. 1908. It was occasionally known as Traynor's Pond for Patrick Traynor, who used it to supply his ice business. The outlet near Broad Street controlled the level of the pond, but its spillway was unable to handle heavy rains and often contributed to flooding (see p. 76).

Triangle Park, c. 1910. In 1906 the town established its first park between Walnut Street and the junction of Mountain and Lawrence Avenues. The house to the right is 300 Mountain Avenue, and partially hidden to the left of it is the Reeve House, the future home of the Westfield Historical Society.

Lawrence and Mountain Avenues, c. 1920. The beautiful Victorian homes on Walnut Street are still there. The house just to the right of the cannon was featured as an example of Neo-Jacobean styling in Westfield artist Harry Devlin's book *To Grandfather's House We Go*.

Park on Mountain Avenue.   WESTFIELD, N. J.

The Park on Mountain Avenue, c. 1910. The cannon, reputed to be a relic of the Civil War, was removed at least partially due to complaints that the area had no historical military significance. (Baumann)

Triangle Park, c. 1925. The tree that at one time nearly obscured the view of the park is now one of the tallest in the area.

VIEW IN MINDOWASKER PARK, Westfield, N. J.

Mindowaskin Park, *c.* 1919. After years of debate, the town finally made the commitment to develop the park. At the dedication, on Sunday, June 1, 1918, it was named "Min-do-was-kin," after one of the four Indian chiefs who deeded the lands now comprising northern New Jersey.

YOUNGSTERS FISHING IN MINDOWASKIN PARK, WESTFIELD, N. J.

Youngsters Fishing, *c.* 1922. The name Mindowaskin initially caused some problems, especially for postcard publishers, who rushed cards into print with no less than four different spellings! In his *History of Westfield,* Charles A. Philhower, who had chosen the name, carefully explains its origin and pronunciation.

Youngsters Fishing, *c.* 1922. Fishing is a timeless recreation.

Overlooking Mindowaskin Park, *c.* 1927. The rebuilt dam—with an enlarged spillway, together with a system of storm sewers in the business district—alleviated the flooding problems that had plagued the town for decades. A pleasant bonus is the little terrace that provides a place to rest and view the pond.

Swans Returning from the End of the Lake, *c.* 1920s. For many years a fixture at the park, the swans swim by the graceful arched bridge, one of the park's landmarks.

Mindowaskin Park, *c.* 1920s. Always a favorite of photographers, the swans and their cygnets glide by one of the islands.

56

Mindowaskin Park, *c.* 1922. This unusual view looks across the pond toward the spillway, E. Broad Street, and St. Paul Street. (PVH)

"One Group at Lunch Time," *c.* 1920s. This popular image was used by at least four different postcard publishers over a twenty-year period.

A View of Mindowaskin Park, c. 1925. This unusual view, looking out from inside the park, shows the circle and the exit leading to Euclid Avenue, as well as the houses on Euclid. (PVH)

Mindowaskin Park, c. 1925. This photograph was taken from a spot near the Mountain Avenue entrance looking down toward the arched bridge. Today mature trees block the view of the bridge.

Mindowaskin Park, East Drive, *c.* 1925. This view toward the eastern shore is from the overlook by the spillway.

The Stairs to Mountain Avenue, *c.* 1925. Very few improvements to the town's infrastructure have been accomplished without some degree of controversy. In hindsight, the vast majority have proven to be sound long-range investments providing significant returns.

The Waterwheel, *c.* 1925. In 1810 Henry Baker built a gristmill near the present-day Mill Lane. For many years visitors to Echo Lake Park enjoyed the waterwheel near the old dam.

Echo Lake, near Westfield, N.J.

2803

Echo Lake, *c.* 1907. The mill property, including Echo Lake, was sold to Ezra Parkhurst by William Darby in 1851. The farm on the bluffs overlooking the lake was acquired by the Cranford Golf Club in 1911 and eventually became the Echo Lake Country Club.

The Drive to Echo Lake Park, *c.* 1925. Union County has more park acreage per capita than any other county in the country. In 1924 it bought the Parkhurst Farm and additional land upstream. The county created a second lake and cut through a drive from Mountain Avenue to Springfield Avenue.

Feeding the Ducks, *c.* 1925. The park's graceful drive along its two lakes has always provided bird watchers with opportunities to observe a variety of migratory birds and waterfowl.

The Pavilion, Echo Lake Park, c. 1925. The park, which straddles the boundary between Westfield and Mountainside, complements the town's recreational facilities.

Echo Lake Park
Westfield, N. J.

Echo Lake Park, c. 1925. Echo Lake has provided a wide range of athletic facilities as well as picnic areas, fishing in season, and boating. In winter the hills are used for sledding; when the weather permits, ice skating is available as well.

The "Osborn Elm", *c.* 1906. This house, which had been recently completed by Dr. Theodore Harvey, replaced Thomas Baker's Inn and Tavern. The house and tree were removed to permit the construction of the movie theater on the corner of E. Broad Street and Central Avenue. (PVH)

Tamaques Park, East End, *c.* 1938. Like Mindowaskin, Tamaques Park was named after an Indian chief. It was by no means the last of Westfield's parks, but it was the last within the postcard era, and added much-needed recreational and athletic facilities.

The Sentinels, Westfield, N. J.

1519

Dear Gertie — How do you like our new postals? all well here
Aunt Alice

The Sentinels, *c.* 1906. Scenery such as this helped attract the Biograph film company to Westfield. During 1910 and 1911 they shot seven movies starring Mary Pickford in and around Westfield.

Six

Mountainside

Westfield Avenue, Mountainside, N.J.

Westfield Avenue, Mountainside, c. 1906. Unhappy that their taxes were paying for a fire department, electric street lights, and new sewers in the village of Westfield that they would never benefit from, the taxpayers of Locust Grove, Branch Mills, and Baltusrol formed the borough of Mountainside in 1895.

The Children's Country Home, c. 1905. This was originally the home of John Drew. As children, John, Lionel, and Ethel Barrymore frequently visited their uncle here. A group representing Westfield's churches incorporated the Children's Country Home in 1893 as a summer respite for underprivileged children and purchased the Drew estate in 1896.

The Children's Country Home, c. 1910. The first crippled children were accepted in 1897. In 1910 a wing was added and the front was modified. It continued to grow, and in 1922 was converted to a year-round facility. Now known as the Children's Specialized Hospital, it is one of the leading institutions of its kind in the world. (Baumann)

Children at the Country Home, *c.* 1918. A group of children pose on the lawn with one of their nurses. Over the years the hospital has played a leading role in the treatment of cerebral palsy and polio as well as in the rehabilitation of spinal cord and other injuries. It has always benefited from wide support within the Westfield community. (WHS)

The Schoolhouse, *c.* 1906. Although a separate borough, Mountainside remained a part of Westfield's educational system until this school was built in 1904. (Baumann)

The Memorial Home for Orphans, c. 1906. Dr. J. Ackerman Coles, in memory of his mother and aunt, donated this large hilltop house to the Newark Orphan Asylum as a summer home for city children. (Baumann)

The Lake at the Memorial Home, c. 1910. The donation included about 20 acres of farmland, orchards, and woods, as well as a brook along what is now Route 22. When this photograph was taken children spent six months a year there. Later on, into the 1940s, the summer period ran from the end of June to the opening of school in September.

The Chapel at Branch Mills, *c.* 1905. The outgrowth of a Sunday school dating from 1825, this stone chapel, an adjunct of the Westfield Presbyterian Church, was built on Springfield Avenue in 1901. In the late 1940s it was sold to the congregation of the Church of Christ and functions today as the Christadelphian Chapel. (WHS)

The Mountainside Chapel, *c.* 1906. Known as the Locust Grove Union Chapel, this church was built in 1901 on Springfield Avenue near Mountain Avenue. As traffic increased, the road became Route 29 and then Route 22. The abandoned chapel was left stranded between the east and west lanes of the highway and was eventually demolished. (Baumann)

TOWER HOUSE
MOUNTAINSIDE
WESTFIELD, N. J.

Tower House, c. 1906. This house, located on what is now Route 22, not far from Echo Lake, gave its name to the Tower Steak House, which has been recently torn down to make way for a large movie theater.

Westfield Nurseries, c. 1905. In 1893 Theodore A. Ball started a nursery near the corner of Mountain and Springfield Avenues. In addition to flowers and plants, he sold a wide variety of ornamental shrubs and trees, many of which enhanced the beautiful homes of this area. He served as Mountainside's postmaster until 1911.

Seven

Events

The Casino Fire of 1911. On the morning of December 6, a fire broke out in a small room near the furnace in the basement of the Casino. An employee smelled smoke, found the fire, and ran to Elm Street to telephone the fire department. By that time the entire building was ablaze. (PVH)

Battling the Casino Blaze. Within minutes firemen were training two hoses from the brand new Webb Pumper on the inferno. At the time, Hugh Platt, who now lives on Wychwood Road, was walking with a friend to the Prospect School from his home at the corner of Kimball and Lawrence Avenues. (WHS)

A Gathering of Spectators. Seeing the smoke, and, as they reached Elm Street, the fire hoses, the boys ran to the site dragging the sleds they had hoped to use on the newly fallen snow. They joined a growing crowd observing the fruitless efforts to save the Casino. The year before, Hugh had been a pupil in Grace Phillip's private kindergarten held in the Casino's basement. (WHS)

The Casino's Demise. It wasn't long before the fire had burned through the roof, leaving only the rafters and chimney showing. The Webb Pumper, however, was credited with preventing the wind from carrying the fire next door to the parsonage of the Baptist church. (WML)

Inspecting the Ruins. Even before the ruins had cooled sufficiently to permit a careful inspection, it was evident that the Casino was a total loss. (WHS)

President William Howard Taft campaigned in Westfield for the Republican re-nomination on May 24, 1912. (WHS)

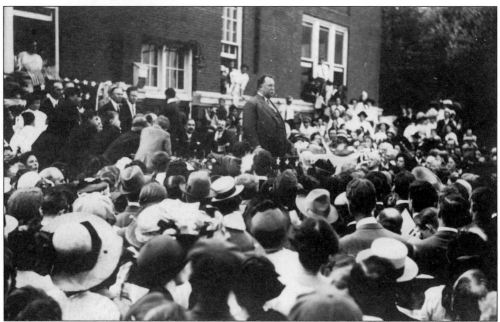

Speaking in front of Washington School, he reminded his audience that his opponent, former president Theodore Roosevelt, had supported him for the presidency just a few years before. (WHS)

T.R. spoke at the same site the next day advocating economic and social reform. He won most of the primaries and the popular vote, but on June 12, 1912, the Republican convention nominated Taft. (WHS)

Charging that Taft had stolen the nomination, Roosevelt ran against him on the ticket of the hastily formed Progressive Party. With the Republican Party split, the Democratic Party's candidate, Woodrow Wilson, won the presidency. (WHS)

The Flood on August 4, 1915. Westfield was accustomed to floods after heavy rains. This one put Prospect, Elm, North, and Broad all under water. Businesses found their basements flooded. The trolley was forced to stop at Dudley, and commuters had to take horse-drawn cabs to the train station. Storm sewers to carry the water to South Avenue eventually solved the annual problem.

Welcome Home, October 12, 1919. Four years later the intersection of Broad and Elm was all decked out with bunting in tribute to the men and women returning from service in World War I. (WHS)

The Trust Co., October 12, 1919. Westfield's citizens have demonstrated their patriotic spirit on many public occasions. The Welcome Home activities have been described as the "greatest celebration" of the war. This should be no surprise: out of a total population of less than 9,000, nearly 500 had seen war service in some capacity. (WHS)

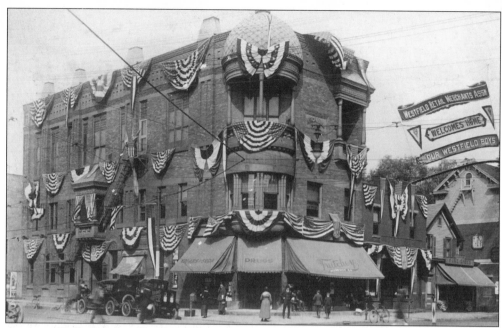

Arcanum Hall, October 12, 1919. The sign over the street at Elm and Broad reads "Westfield Retail Merchants Assn. Welcomes Home Our Westfield Boys." Next door was the Gas Company and then Silberg's shoe store. The building furthest to the right was the Westfield Inn. (WHS)

Broad Street, October 12, 1919. Julius Lusardi lived above his candy store at 152 E. Broad Street. Next door, E.L. Saunders decorated both his pool hall and his cigar store. The roof line on the two buildings has now been unified. Otherwise their appearance has changed very little. (WHS)

R.M. French & Son's Store, October 12, 1919. Robert M. and R. Warren French moved their furniture business into a brand new building in January 1913. Although no longer a furniture store, the building can be seen today on the corner of Elm Street and North Avenue. (WHS)

The R.M. French & Son Float, October 12, 1919. The actual festivities of the day began with a gala parade. The local merchants, most of whom lived in or near Westfield, gave it their whole-hearted support. (WHS)

Welcome Home, October 12, 1919. This float was sponsored by one of the churches. (WHS)

The Merchants Association Float, October 12, 1919. The merchants used this float to commemorate the role played by the township's traders during the Revolutionary War. The photograph was taken on Orchard Street, which was one of the parade's assembly points. (WHS)

The Welcome Home Parade, October 12, 1919. This float was made by the Children's Sewing Society. (WHS)

The Welcome Home Parade, October 12, 1919. Children from the Prospect Sewing Circle are shown here. (WHS)

The Plaza, October 12, 1919. The parade terminated at the plaza, where an estimated crowd of 20,000—more than double the town's population—gathered to watch the parade and see the troops pass in review. At one end of the plaza a temporary memorial arch had been erected. (WHS)

The Memorial Arch, October 12, 1919. The names of the eighteen local men who gave their lives in the war effort were inscribed on the arch. At night it was lit up as part of "a prodigious electrical display with fireworks, music, dancing, and public speaking. Many of the heroes of the war were pictured in electrical outline." (WHS)

A Review of the Troops, October 12, 1919. A large panoramic photograph was taken of the assembled troops. Small portions of the center section of the image were used to create postcards. One of the original photographs now hangs in the Westfield Historical Society. (WHS)

Detail. Martin Wallberg enlisted with the Canadian forces in 1915 because "he felt it was his duty to do so." In 1917, ordered to advance, he thrust his bayonet through the silk American flag that he had just received from Westfield, "and went over the top with the colors flying—to death and everlasting glory." The flag was returned to Westfield. (WHS)

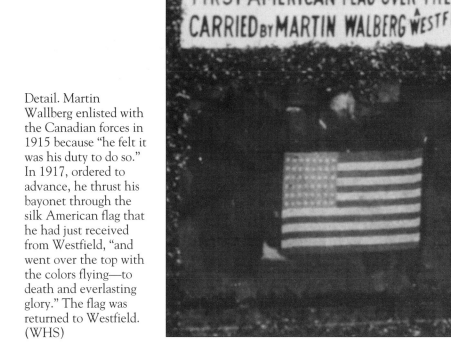

North Avenue, October 12, 1919. Sponsored by the Westfield Fire Department, the sign over the street reads "Welcome Home Boys. We honor you for going. We are glad you are back." (WHS)

The Firehouse, October 12, 1919. (WHS)

Eight
Winter Scenes

East Broad Street, 1914. If recent winters have seemed unusually harsh, following as they have a number of mild years, it would be wise to remember that weather is cyclic. The storm on March 1, 1914, was described as the worst since the Blizzard of 1888. If it were not for the library, this snow-clogged street would probably be unrecognizable. (WHS)

Elm Street, 1914. Even under 22 inches of snow there is no mistaking Elm Street. Over the years the town has learned how to minimize disruption of business due to the weather. The horses entering the scene to the right are probably pulling a sleigh. By 1935 snow was hauled away by trucks.

Storm Damage, March 2, 1914. The weight of the snow and ice on the wires was too much for the poles west of the train station. The Tuttle Brothers coal and lumber yard is to the left of the tracks beyond the grade crossing. The girders between the tracks mark the trolley underpass. (Baumann/WHS)

Swans in Winter, *c. 1922.* Theodore Hintz, a local photographer, captured the beautiful side of nature with this image of the swans by the snow-covered bridge in Mindowaskin Park. (Photograph by Theodore Hintz)

Mindowaskin Park, 1922. Another view, probably by the same photographer, shows the swans swimming through the reflection of the snow-covered trees. (WHS)

The Presbyterian Church in Winter. Churches seem to be especially photogenic when surrounded by snow. (Groff, Scotch Plains)

Skaters on the Pond, c. 1907. Winter provides recreation as well. The sender waited until the warmth of June to send this message to "Anna Wittke, Broad Street, Town." It reads "I don't see you anywhere, either on the ice or in church, but I know you are used to visiting at both places."

The Episcopal Church in Winter, *c.* 1906.

The Congregational Church in Winter, *c.* 1906.

A Winter View of 519 Highland Avenue. Private homes, as well as churches, have a special snow-covered beauty.

A Photographic Postcard of 703 Highland Avenue. For many years, individuals could have ordinary rolls of film printed on postcard-backed paper.

Nine

Downtown

The Town Hall, *c.* 1911. Originally built in 1906 as a home for the *Union County Standard*, a second floor was added and it was leased to the town in 1910. It was eventually purchased and functioned as the municipal building and police headquarters until 1954. A new front makes it difficult to visualize the building at 111 Prospect Street. (WML)

Broad Street, *c.* 1906. The sign by the curb reads "Louis Dughi, Crane's Philadelphia Ice Cream. Soda Water Made From Real Fruit Flavors." Today the balconies on the building with the arched front no longer protrude over the sidewalk, but the buildings appear otherwise unchanged.

Broad Street, *c.* 1911. Dughi's building is at the far left of the intersection. At the near left, Casey's sign advertises Fritz's Ice Cream. Out of sight, to the right of the photographer, was Louis Glasser's store. Near that, on the corner, was The Peoples National Bank.

The Peoples National Bank, *c.* 1911. The bank began business in 1907 and moved into this building at the corner of Broad and Prospect Streets in 1910. Having previously changed its name to The People's Bank and Trust Company, in early 1923 it moved into larger quarters at the corner of Elm Street and North Avenue.

Prospect Street, *c.* 1907. This was the scene looking up Prospect Street from in front of the fire department. In the distance on the right is the Dughi building on E. Broad Street. The building on the corner to the left was the home of the *Union County Standard*, the competitor of the *Westfield Leader*. It is now gone, as is the corner building on the right. (PVH)

Westfield Fire Department, Westfield, N. J.

The Fire Department, *c.* 1911. The Westfield Fire Department was incorporated in 1883 by two representatives each from the Westfield Hook and Ladder Co., the Bucket and Engine Co., and the Empire Engine Co. In 1903 this became the town's fire department. Land for the original frame building was purchased in 1887. An example of Moorish-style architecture, the present fire department headquarters was formally opened in May 1911. Fire hoses were hung in the building's tower to dry so they would not rot. The first alarm consisted of ringing the Prospect Street School bell. Later a steel locomotive tire rim was installed in a lot on Elm Street. That proved to be insufficient and a committee, after four years of deliberations, chose to build a 75-foot steel tower at the rear of the firehouse. The fire bell on the top of the tower remained in service from the mid-1890s until 1939, when it was replaced by an air horn on the roof of the firehouse. (PVH)

North Avenue and Elm, *c.* 1907. Next to the firehouse was a small park in front of the train station. This picture was taken from the park looking up Elm Street. On the left corner of North Avenue and Elm Street was the Home Building and Supply Co., which was responsible for the construction of many of the houses of that era.

A Home Building and Supply Co. Advertising Postcard. As the town grew several streets had to be renumbered. Harrison Avenue was one of them. (WML)

95

ELM STREET, WESTFIELD, N. J.

8.24-06

Hot weather here

C. H. N.

Elm Street, 1906. Just opposite Quimby Street was Karl Baumann's Photo Studio. He was probably responsible for the images on at least one-half of Westfield's early postcards. In 1911 he relocated to E. Broad Street and, shortly after, the post office's building replaced his one-story frame studio.

Post Office, Westfield, N. J.

The Post Office, c. 1912. The train station brought ever increasing traffic to Elm Street, and business began to concentrate here. The National Bank of Westfield opened in the post office's building on March 2, 1912, and stayed until 1918. To the left, J.V. Marsh advertised "Boy Scout shoes for your son." Above the bank a sign read "Law Offices. Frederick B. Taggert."

96

The Post Office's Building, *c.* 1917. The bank advertised "Foreign Exchange, Letters of Credit, Travelers Checks, and Safe Deposit Boxes." In 1919 the Central Union Council of the Boy Scouts of America, under the leadership of John D. McEwen, located in the building. The building remains but the balcony and the columns are gone.

Hutchinson's Store, *c.* 1910. Across Elm Street, close to E. Broad Street, Hutchinson's Store moved into Patrick Traynor's old building in 1907.

The Trust Company's Building, *c*. 1905. Until 1892 the southwest corner of Elm and E. Broad was empty. Children used it to play ball, and once a year the circus pitched its tents on the lot. In 1893 the First National Bank of Westfield was constructed on the site. In 1903 the name was changed to The Westfield Trust Company.

Broad Street, *c*. 1907. A sign in the upper window reads "Atlas Lodge #125—F.&A. M.," which met here from 1894 until the Masonic Temple was built in 1929. The post office shared the first floor with the bank. Luther M. Whitaker was the postmaster.

The Westfield Trust Company, 1912. The flourishing bank outgrew its facilities by 1911 and underwent a major renovation the next year. The entire upper portion of the building was raised 8 feet, windows were enlarged to provide natural lighting, and a revolving door was added. The post office moved to Elm Street at this time.

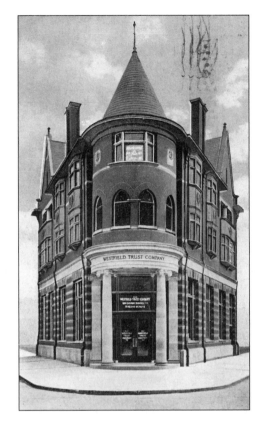

Bank Square, c. 1930. The constant flooding took its toll; the bank was completely rebuilt and looks today as it did then.

Arcanum Hall, *c.* 1906. In this view, taken before the fire, the Casino is barely visible on Elm Street. The first floor of Arcanum Hall was occupied by George W. Frutchey's drug store and soda shop. The balcony over the side door has since been removed.

Arcanum Hall, *c.* 1912. By this time the Casino had burned and the Westfield Theater had been built. In addition to the pharmacy, Frutchey had a real estate business. With Harry Schaefer, he published a series of postcards that sold in his store and promoted his real estate. Baumann did their photography.

Wittke's Corner, *c*. 1905. Charles Wittke owned a stationery and tobacco shop on the corner of Elm and E. Broad Streets. The building looks the same today. Patrick Traynor's grocery store was on the right. In 1906 a gas explosion damaged the basement of Traynor's store and the next year Hutchinson's Store moved into the premises (see p. 97).

Elm Street from Broad, 1908. This postcard, addressed to Ed Wittke, shows Scheuer's Market, diagonally opposite Wittke's Corner. Later it became Wohlfert's Hardware Store. In 1918 the National Bank of Westfield (see p. 96) purchased the site, and a bank has been located on the corner ever since.

A View from Mountain Avenue, c. 1912. This image shows Elmer Street, the library, and the Westfield Dairy to its right. (Baumann/PVH)

The Public Library, 1906. At the time this photograph was taken, construction was not quite finished. The lamp posts were not yet in place on the top of the steps, and the landscaping along the walk was incomplete. Today the building has wings on either side and is most easily recognized from the rear.

Elmer Street, *c.* 1911. The Congregational church is to the left. Most of the houses on the right are no longer there.

Broad Street and Mountain Avenue, *c.* 1908. Samuel Downer had a general store in this house in the early 1800s. It was bought by Westfield physician Adrian C. Kinch in 1850, and his son, Dr. Frederick A. Kinch, remodeled it into this beautiful Victorian home.

G.O. Keller, *c.* 1940s. One of the older businesses in Westfield, even the name on this E. Broad Street building remains the same. (PVH)

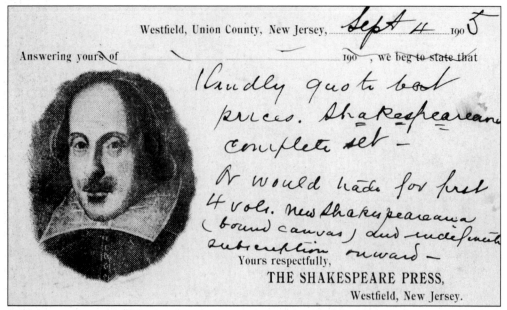

Shakespeare Press, 1905. Located in the *Union County Standard* building at the corner of North Avenue and Prospect Street (see p. 93), the company concentrated on educational, dramatic, and genealogical works. They were also the printers for the Shakespeare Society of New York. (PVH)

Ten

Around Town

First Street, c. 1908. Westfield has always been a town of beautiful homes and wide tree-lined streets. This is one of the cards published by Schaefer and Frutchey, in part to promote their real estate interests.

Westfield Avenue from Park Street, 1911.

Westfield Avenue, *c.* 1906.

Westfield Avenue, *c.* 1920.

Summit Avenue, *c.* 1905.

The Boulevard, *c.* 1906.

The Boulevard, Westfield, N. J.

I received your letter and will write soon. With love from Han—

The Boulevard, *c.* 1905.

The Boulevard from Park Street, *c.* 1911. (PVH)

Carlton Place and Park Street, *c.* 1905.

Park Street and Carlton Avenue, *c.* 1910.

Carlton Place, *c.* 1905.

Fairfield Circle and Carlton Road, *c*. 1910.

Carlton Road, *c*. 1911.

Entrance to Stoneleigh Park, Westfield, N. J. 1518

The Entrance to Stoneleigh Park, *c*. 1906. Stoneleigh Park is one of the first examples in the region of a completely enclosed, exclusive community with deed restrictions controlled by an incorporated home owner's association. (Baumann)

A General View of Stoneleigh Park, *c*. 1906. At the time Karl Baumann took these photographs, most of the trees were quite young. Today they provide a good deal of shade in the summer, an abundant supply of leaves in the fall, and are attractive year round. (Baumann)

The Main Entrance of Stoneleigh Park, *c.* 1906. (Baumann)

Stoneleigh Park's Entrance from Westfield Avenue, *c.* 1906. (Baumann)

New York Avenue, *c.* 1908. Now called Trinity Place, the old Holy Trinity Church is no longer here, but the house to the right with the twin towers remains. (Schaefer and Frutchey)

South Avenue, *c.* 1908. This picture was taken at about the 800 block looking toward Scotch Plains.

Stanley Avenue, *c.* 1920. Looking from E. Broad Street, the front walk to Grant School is on the right. Arlington Avenue had not yet been developed at this time. The houses in the distance are on Lenox Avenue.

Hillcrest Avenue, *c.* 1920.

Tremont Avenue, *c.* 1912.

Lenox Avenue, *c.* 1912.

Lenox Avenue, *c.* 1925. (Schaefer and Frutchey)

Lenox Avenue, *c.* 1908.

Euclid Avenue, *c.* 1906.

Euclid Avenue, *c.* 1908. (Schaefer and Frutchey)

Dr. J.J. Hogan's Residence, *c.* 1923. The house is located on Euclid Avenue across the street from the Women's Club. Dr. Hogan was listed in the town directory for only two years.

N. Euclid Avenue at the Corner of E. Broad Street, *c.* 1912. (Baumann)

Stanley Oval, *c.* 1912. (Baumann)

Elm Street, *c.* 1907. Dr. Chauncey Egel, a dentist who served as president of the board of education, lived in this home, which was eventually demolished to make way for a supermarket. A pond on his property across Elm Street was filled in when Washington School was built. It is now part of the soccer field.

Harrison Avenue, *c.* 1906.

Harrison Avenue. (PVH)

Wychwood, the South Gate, *c.* 1935. Planned as an exclusive community with unique homes designed for gracious country living, Wychwood was the innovative housing development of Arthur Rule. Many of the historical houses were moved to Wychwood from other towns.

Wonder House. Designed by Bernhardt E. Muller and built by Arthur R. Rule, this "six-room French-Norman cottage" was reconstructed in Westfield where it became the "South Gate" at Wychwood and the residence of Arthur Rule Jr.

Highland Avenue, *c*. 1912. (Baumann)

Kimball Avenue, *c*. 1906.

Alden Avenue, *c*. 1930.

Sinclair Place, *c*. 1930.

A Photographic Postcard of 426 Birch Avenue, c. 1920.

Mountain Avenue, just above Walnut Street, c. 1908. (Schaefer and Frutchey)

Prospect Street from Dudley Avenue, *c.* 1910. (PVH)

Prospect Street, at Its Intersection with Walnut Avenue, *c.* 1908. (Schaefer and Frutchey)

Dudley Avenue from Elm Street, *c*. 1906.

Dudley Avenue from Prospect Street.

Bibliography

Hershey, Jean Hesketh. *History of the Borough of Mountainside*. Mountainside, NJ: n.p., 1976.

Hylan, Robert C. *First Congregational Church*. Westfield, NJ: First Congregational Church, 1980.

Hoffman, Robert V. *The Olde Towne*. Westfield: Robert V. Hoffman, 1937.

Johnson, James P. *Westfield: From Settlement to Suburb*. Westfield, NJ: Westfield Bicentennial Committee, 1976.

McKinney, William K., Chas. A. Philhower, and Harry A. Kniffen. *Commemorative History of the Presbyterian Church*. 1929.

Pearsall, Herbert J. *A History of Westfield*. Westfield, NJ: *The Westfield Leader*, 1935.

Philhower, Charles A. *History of the Town of Westfield*. New York: Lewis Historical Publishing Company, 1923.

The Westfield Historical Manuscripts Collection. (Vertical files.)

The Westfield Leader. (1907–present, on microfilm.)

The Library, *c.* 1908. All of the materials listed in the bibliography can be found in the Local History Room of the Westfield Memorial Library.